Inconsistencies

Mireille Kamrowski

BookLeaf Publishing

Presentation by *BookLeaf Publishing*

Web: www.bookleafpub.com

E-mail: info@bookleafpub.com

ISBN: 978-93-95890-42-7

First edition 2022

To anyone who knows who they are when they read my poetry or finds meaning within it.

ACKNOWLEDGEMENT

In the order of viewing every life lesson as a blessing, there is much to be grateful for. I would like to mention that despite any relationship I have with those who may have become absent in my life, my father was the one person who always believed I could write, and tried to harbour my love for it, even in times that I couldn't. My family (as a whole) has provided lots of inspiration for the words I have found, in the strangest of times, where I would desperately search for a pen or paper, or hope that my cell phone had enough of a charge to be able to open the notes app and let everything out. So for that, I am thankful.

PREFACE

In 2004 someone important once read a school project of mine that set off a life long dream and appreciation for writing, that was eventually, and inevitably, discouraged. This personal project was a long time coming, and a big 'F-YOU' to those who have decided to disregard and throw away the love I have for this, the love I have for them, and the love I have wanted back as well. With all changes in life, now is as good a time as any to give in to my dreams and release this to the world unapologetically.

Only My Father

I have changed quite simply
from when I was young,
and in other ways not at all.
I wrote as a child,
I made art as a child,
and grade school teachers asked my dreams.
I told everyone I'd keep doing this;
making small unpublishable books,
with stapled pages displaying bees and
rainbows,
always checking the spelling with Mom,
happy to show you after a day at work.
I told you my eyes wished they had shutters,
you allowed it through disposable film,
and taught me to shoot.
New photos of old places to get me to write.
I personified train stations,
songs I was too embarrassed to sing,
and then, again, when your mother died.
I wrote for everyone I loved,
and for a while it seemed you loved it too.
Encouragement felt stifling at times,
there's a frustration towards my complacency;
unfinished passions, and certification.
I promised you I'd find my place,

perhaps in a box if it made me feel loved.
This poetry isn't that good,
and neither am I.
There will always be a different meaning,
after every discussion and disagreement.
I have drawn on the walls,
and permanently on the skin you gave me-
knowing my words tattooed your heart also,
telling you maybe Plath died for our sins,
hurting you the way kids hurt parents,
or possibly worse,
the way I view it as worse for me as well,
while parents idealize hobbies and interests.
Somehow still you see me being classic,
emotional and hopeless like Hemingway,
you must be the only person who thinks I'm a
writer.

Inconsistencies

I never claimed to be a green witch,
I don't worship nature as a daughter,
or anything else I was taught to believe.
You can keep asking if I pray,
and when I do I will try to remember you,
In the dark, these thoughts are my own,
intrusive and unwielding I keep learning,
about maybe myself and yourself as well.
I am afraid of the hidden insects,
but especially the ones I can see.
Still with your gluttonous heavy food,
and fake health that you show me,
I do end up craving the taste of chlorophyll,
and the earthy smell of forests,
I used to pick flowers for people I love,
bittersweet about them sitting in water,
only to get added to the bags in the dump.
I am, unfortunately, a city girl,
walking in malls more often than parks.
Verdure I've grown sits in my house,
and the summertime pots on my patio,
while I do as well in denial,
I'm not allowed into this coven,
killing plants in my suburban routines.
Ignorant to cycles other than mine,

failing at adapting everyday,
my own laziness breaks for coffee,
and always some time for TV.
I've come to hold expectation for years,
I have part of hardship's relativity,
I am a woman with fears,
(and pain, and hopes, and dreams)
as well as my inconsistencies.

Cement Sun

Summer wind makes petals fall,
whispering like the initial soft snow-
the kind the dog likes to play in.
Branches stretch and knot,
budding twigs take shape for homes,
nature makes sounds in peace;
there is no struggle outside.
Dandelion wishes don't apologize,
life settles where it's been placed,
without question there is growth.
Naked freshness sits in the grass,
allowing gentle paw prints to show,
from dew to the start of pavement,
the cement sun burns our bare feet;
a masochism we indulge each year.
This heat isn't a long enough season,
always far gone by All Saint's Day;
but we don't visit the graves anymore,
even my birthday is forgotten,
so after all of the candy and dress-up,
the summer sky becomes heavy concrete,
blankets of white no longer smell floral.

No Filter

Nostalgia was there,
in every thunderstorm,
ruining all the picnic plans,
with the familiar flashes and claps,
like closing your eyes in front of the camera;
ruining what you tried to make,
the storm cleaned half the city,
only the damp was left the next morning,
followed always with a vibrant sky.
Your stomach hurt that night,
but the orange and bronze,
it settled in your bones,
like the dog sunbathing and warm,
making you think of childhood,
bowls of sherbet and smiles.
But in the spring, colour can retire,
telling you it may rain again,
the same way a polaroid appears,
the weather of feeling as nearly instantaneous.
You can picture yourself a meaningful person,
capture it on film and edit the saturation.
That blue house you lived in looked grey,
but there was no filter on anything yet,
to prove that these ghosts exist.
You would deny them anyway,

dressed in your finest floral linens,
that were folded messily away.
Though it's funny you've developed,
and grown too big for your frame,
the faded place still exists,
with sun bleaching and cancers,
you'll always remember that honest exposure.

Hiding

When you live in row housing,
you can smell your neighbour's cooking,
the laundry from two doors down,
you, and especially your dog, can hear
everything-
even the ghosts.
She barks when people knock on the door,
sometimes, for fun, I knock on my hip bone.
The thought of someone outside,
is frightening and exciting;
I've been hiding myself inside my house.

When you live in a body,
you can feel plush carpet under your feet,
a pulsing heart rate after going upstairs,
you, and especially your husband, can feel love-
even in silence.
He's comfortable without having to talk,
sometimes, while quiet, I hold a point on my
shoulder,
the thought of bones as visible on the outside,
is terrifying and entrancing.
I've been hiding a skeleton inside my body.

Bath and Bordeaux

Plath wrote that bathtubs heal everything,
but hot water soaks through all of my flesh,
and only leaves boredom in thought;
making me heavier when I step on the scale.
People have baths that look like water-colour,
they emerge youthful and unstained after some
time.
I tried to sit in some pastel hues,
hoping the water was like glass,
and that happiness would come from a rosy tone.
My hair was the colour of Bordeaux,
but it didn't seem intoxicating,
it's not quite long enough to choke you;
I'm not a siren that can make you show passion,
and when I put my head under, colour leeches
out.
the bath turns my hair into petals that blush at
my body,
but that water doesn't taste like wine.
Even when diluted it never feels light,
it leaves my skin plump with my insides heavy,
and even though the excess wrinkles and falls,
I feel I'll never fully dissolve,
I wonder how to become both the solvent and
solution.

Eccentricites

My childhood eccentricities haunt me,
calling an adult's comments sarcastic,
where did that knowing confidence go?
If I imagine myself as calm and content,
having a coffee, watching re-runs on tv,
the same thing as always,
to convince my eyelids into sleep.
My house is warmly weighted with blankets,
decorated for a stranger's appeal,
all the while aiming for recognition,
I claim to be something special,
'one day my name will be known',
my imagination sees my aspirations,
I am no artist, but what if I was?
Everything pleasing is mediocre,
I have talents only stretching so far,
endeavors too scary to follow,
turning around and always knowing,
yet silently thinking I'm somehow better,
my God complex will always propel me,
no one hates me more than I can,
my hubris is not uncommonly aberrant,
I am still here doing and moving,
not wanting to explain ambiguous writing,
or who I am between those I know.

I'll be that unknown with quiet pretension,
pleased, but sad, when there is time for it,
as my loved and natural default,
that therapy would only rid me of.
So I struggle and thrive,
purposefully and cyclically,
every version getting formulated,
unorthodox and unapologetic as I go.

Aquarius

The doctor always knows what's best,
they blame you or assure you it's never your fault,
but they were quiet when they rushed,
I already knew from the air holding uncertainty.
I loved you when my womb gave up having a place for you,
when I knew I'd never hold you or see your face.
I never felt you- it was too early,
but I knew you were there.
I had seen you on a screen- you had a shimmering heart,
it blinked so quickly in front of me.
You became a constellation;
Aqaurius.
I tattooed myself with those stars in alignment,
it was the only trace left of you.
I wished the seedling you were could've blossomed,
so you became the tiniest forget-me-not,
telling me I could move on.
I didn't know it then, but 14 weeks aged me.
Every stress brought by more anxiety.
I couldn't process enough to name you,
Aquarius,

so they named you 'debris';
and with that a name for this chapter in my life.
It was called remorse and resentment,
and even superstition,
something as simple as black cats and ladders.
A nurse told me you were a plant in a garden,
the first tomato that sprouted and flowered,
only to stop because surrounding weeds
suffocate.
Nature will test itself with a storm,
but there were no pests inside of me,
just my karma preventing you from getting
strong.
'All life is like that', I'm told and I read,
sometimes water can even burn leaves
when the midday sunshine gets hot,
both essential, both equally devastating.
Well, I know that now and I know the pain
readied me;
I had so much ugliness then- inadequate without
you,
purposeless and numb that I had never known.
I still fear the worst everyday as I should have
before,
sometimes I lay awake sweating and waiting.
I place my hands where you were,
where your sister is now.
She will never know you and neither will I,

I hope you'd have loved me as much as I feared you,
Aquarius,
I'm sorry my body couldn't make you a home.

I'm Evergreen

My body isn't a place I find rest in,
I tell myself kind lies with forced quiet,
I do have comfort in my mother's words,
she's told me that I've shed my skin.
Every week I rebuild who I've been,
while scrubbing tree sap from my hands,
with continuous growth I'd be okay.
Everything touched gathering dust,
eventually falling for mites to explore.
I could never imagine being deciduous,
never changing who I am on the outside,
until the weather tells me its time.
I drop those proverbial leaves each day,
pulling hair from my head and the drain.
Although the seasons do affect me,
growing isn't something that hibernates,
when I've been remade for decades.
I own ugly marks and reminders,
still without trace or stain of anyone,
your skin may not be as thick as bark,
even when you claim nothing hurts,
I will never tell you I'm evergreen.

'Your' Funeral

'Your', a funny sounding word,
the more it gets repeated,
though it was also your surname.
I found myself absent a lot after your death.
'Your' funeral was held quickly,
in dream, and real life as well,
The cathedral was draped in red,
like an opera theatre in wait,
the service now in session,
parishioners in their velvet seats.
You visited me a lot before this,
I thought to myself to ask you,
'What is it like to be dead?'
Only to remind myself,
you were gone, but, a ghost.
Everything you gave me I kept,
especially the dreams;
like seeing you in a casket,
surrounded by photo room red,
I was attending your wake,
I leaned in and you woke,
'Everyone thinks I'm dead,
but I'm here.'
I still don't know what you meant,
but I knew I wasn't feverish.

I wish you'd be more than ashes,
that you'd found a way to survive,
without coming to me in spirit.
I envisioned you face down in pain,
when you were just asleep in bed,
'your' pneumonia caused coffin.
I do forget you sometimes,
but I never need reminding;
every dime I find, and every November,
I feel a bit unfortunate,
with something telling me I'm alive.

Ambition

People wonder where ambition goes as you age,
well, there is no magic answer and no excuse,
it doesn't leave the way you exit a room,
they say you must make use of it before you
forget.
It stays but remains absent from your thoughts;
your memories of using Mom's lipstick on the
wall-
getting tamed by consequence and compromise.
By your parents buying you oil pastels as new
media,
after you've cleaned your abstract from the plain,
they were waxy and bright but slimmer and
stinky.
You'll have 20 creamy colours to choose instead
of red-
the symbol for passion and ambition and
maturity,
red now is remembering what your family
fought for.
Still, you didn't feel like paper or that many
choices,
it was never about the creative expression,
there was a different feeling in mashing that
lipstick

for some reason it's destruction couldn't be satisfying;
the guilt makes you recoil at pink makeup components,
pastels don't feel the same and they're harder to use,
regardless of how open minded the concession.
You may not act with an artist's spirit anymore,
you remember being childlike and less mundane,
imagination is promoted while still being taught,
being an adult means properly placed ambition.

War Paint

What are you and what am I?
We are told we're seen as unrelated.
Older or younger and in different leagues,
you have stolen my accomplishments,
I get to praise them for you and to you.
I have done nothing however,
vapid and empty but somehow still heavy.
I thought I'd always want to fight,
now I tire of hearing I'm young.
I know how to apply myself,
lipsticks and liners and doe eyed lashes;
that's what I'm constructed of.
Jokes of trowels and paint rollers,
this vanity to conceal my ugliness.
Time spent poured into my mirror,
capturing the biggest fear that I see,
reflecting myself and my eyes,
tracing their way up in waking hours,
to transform me with war paint,
quietly and daily in front of me,
a language in colour and brushes,
until my reflection is uncanny and odd.
Your naked face gets fawned over,
through exhaustively picked blemishes,
faultless red in place of blush,

but you don't have time to care,
you were born perfect as you are now,
every line flawlessly out of place,
why should you consider feminine form,
when our comparison is obvious.
Cast your shadow onto me,
make it land on the hollow of my cheeks,
tinting the crease of my eyelids,
and the middle pursing of my lips.
Now I tire of hearing I'm vain.
This fragile face I've refigured everyday,
held together with trend and compliments,
just to feel brave for the day,
trying to figure out how to be you.

Tattoo Artists

What age did you get your first tattoo?
I was too young to know that words were just sounds,
so I let them burrow under my skin,
they're the only quotations I have on my body-
not quite the lyrical motivations others pay for
they aren't black, they're skin coloured-
a perfect match to conceal their meaning.
They start at my toes and go beneath my skull,
and sometimes, before bed, I like to let the artists out.
They find their places again and start sketching their plans on me,
I hear their voices as they etch themselves into position.
"is that your bone?" one asks while patting my calf muscle,
"That's because you're big" one calls out, swinging from my upper arm,
"oh that wont ever go away" says the biggest one, stretching out on my stomach.
Sometimes there are less, sometimes they resign,
it is, after all, hard to make a living as an artist,
when the art is under appreciated.
I lay as still as I can while they work,

eventually the constant needling numbs the
nerves in my skin,
and the buzzing machines lull me to sleep.
In the morning no one else will see all this
invisible ink,
but when someone has,
I wonder what their canvases look like as well,
and what time their tattoo artists come out.

Rainbow Baby

It feels like it could be spring at any time now,
but I don't know for sure from looking out,
the sky is blue with simple stretching clouds,
the sun reflects off my neighbour's windows,
it makes me want to close my curtains,
but my little one loves the light.
I forget she spent those months in darkness,
that every colour and experience is new.
I don't know what it's like to be an infant
but, then again, neither does she.
So the glare comes in and I let myself go blind,
my vision has been tunneled since her birth-
there is nothing more important to me now,
maybe just the rolling toward her toys or the
dog,
and the reaching for prisms on the wall.
This white light so magical to her with its
spectrum,
it's as if she knows she is my rainbow baby,
and that any day the storms could come again,
I could find my days to be black and white,
but God sent us this refraction for our hope.

A Linen Moth

When I saw your skin,
I wondered to myself,
if you'd seen it too,
being youthful and freckled,
but not young or free.
Not quite milky pale,
but still like a linen.
I, drawn in by you,
something like luminance;
a comforting warmth,
felt like nothing but a moth,
breaking you with holes,
and insignificant dust,
from wings that fly,
and hover to your glow.
I've seen this get left,
forgotten in the drawer,
so that you'll get used to me.
I could go there too,
and find rest,
make a home with you,
hoping you're happy.
You're light, and white,
and soft.

And I am too,
but differently.

Horoscope

I weighed my thoughts and mulled over my
name,
this wasn't the first time I'd forgotten who I was,
It has taken a long time to define this, that I am,
I know there are thousands with similar titles as
mine.
My star chart has explained my shortcomings,
I'm adventurous with what I choose to eat,
indecisive about that previous sentence's choice;
charming and cat-like, but don't leave me alone,
impress me with doting and calling me down.
Interesting that everyone on this day senses
solidarity,
yet this communist horoscope feels very
singular.
A fortune teller told me of career as a triple
threat,
I was secure in my heresy of needing to know,
only, she wouldn't allow any foresight of death,
but that I could be old and rich and very in love,
now I sit quietly, using child nap times quickly
to write,

thinking it's important for things to start out dramatic,
It's much easier to close something calm in the end.

Extractions

Teeth; the only 'removable' part of the skeleton,
you could take them all and still survive well,
many turned them into silvery smiles.
I've had my fair share of extractions,
the occasional black hole cavity,
I just learn to chew on the other side,
trying to make sure nothing much falls in,
but I still scrape my tongue obsessively,
endlessly going over one small spot,
while remembering my own negligence.
They say that pregnancy weakens your teeth,
I wonder if I also made my mother's gums bleed.
Sometimes it's caused by something too sweet,
not cleansing after something acidic and sour.
Why do wounds feel so much bigger on the
inside?
Maybe I shouldn't drink coffee like water,
even with that energy I don't rush for fix or
filling.
I had five wisdom teeth that healed in a week,
I'm told that's a meaningful number,
like all the fingers on one hand,
or the age you might start going to school.
I just don't care to use something for sensitivity,
if a tooth is gone it can surely be left or replaced,

precaution is useful when they shift to open
gaps.
It will take a bit of effort and some time,
my gums can mash while I still talk,
the more they rot the more people stay away,
you may have thought of them as necessity,
and even if you believed you would need them,
that doesn't mean they won't leave anyway.

Unnamed Shade

I used to skip lines on loose-leaf paper,
while using the colours in boxes of crayons.
Every other space got filled with orange wax,
A peer showed me if I waved that page fast,
the white and orange would blend together.
'Creamsicle', I thought, 'Peach', he said.
I could taste the vanilla cream inside those blank lines,
it was summer and the treat made my mouth overly cold,
that it soon became warm again.
Those months go by faster as I try to remember,
promising myself I wouldn't forget,
but I have, only my senses take me back,
to winter while helping mom put away groceries.
There were tiny mandarins in boxes,
the buttery peels gave me scented finger prints,
leaving the familiar scent on everything I touched,
like the calendar or phone screen,
to mark my best friend's favourite time of year,
her most beloved child cartoon characters,
bouncing tigers, sarcastic cats and adventurous fish,

now orange also for her baby boy,
as she makes him laugh with toys reminding of nature,
a playful fox that's just a fiery blur in the woods,
as my own child came only 9 months before hers.
My husband calls her a little sweet potato,
and I reply to him, as her voice for now,
playfully saying
'I yam'.
And I am orange too, as I was born in the fall,
every year the stores decorate earlier and earlier for me,
autumnal wreathes and pumpkins lining their shelves,
I crane my neck and reach for that same flavor for coffee as well.
If I'm still and quiet for long enough though,
I feel the vibration of what my body is made of.
The particles of my skin moving, stretching, and growing,
just the same as the white and orange alternating stripes,
from the blueprint of my past,
waving fast enough to turn me peach,
or creamsicle,
or some unnamed shade,
for this rind that covers me,
with fragrant blossoms and noticeable pores,

that propels me to get up in the morning,
and find the meaning in my everyday life.

Gentle Pace

I hope that you speak to yourself in poetry,
and that the teacher voice in your head will blow you away,
with the sounds and beauty of your own thoughts,
making you find your words meaningful again.
I hope when I leave finally,
you'll be able to bid me a fond farewell,
and that the curses you read in your spell books,
stay on closed pages,
with the old clasps somehow holding tight,
making your world peaceful again.
I hope you know that you've been disassociating for years,
and that I don't care if you've passed your trauma down.
I will live with this genetic memory if that's what it is,
sloughing off the dead with sugar and oil so my antlers will grow again,
making you see that you've been impregnated by the devil.
I hope that one day you don't see me as a stranger,

you can tell me all about who is fronting and
who is controlling inside,
every name and age I made you switch,
and forgive me for the ones I don't recall,
making you become one whole person again.
I hope that when you walk outside in the winter,
its not because you're burning up or that you've
forgotten yourself,
I'd prefer you to walk slowly at a gentle pace,
the way my daughter pretends she's a bee
collecting from dandelions,
Making you grateful that broken bones heal
stronger than before.
I hope you age out in your ignorance so that we
both can appeal,
it's better to have differences than to have guilt
for the lies,
I will never beg you again or tell you anything
but the weather,
making it so God knows that it's not forgiven,
but only accepted.
It's the best I can do.

Joyful Mystery

If I were to be positive for once,
I'd say that someone right now is praying a rosary,
the joyful mysteries,
and focusing on the way that every tenth bead ends,
without falling asleep fitfully,
or apologizing to God for stringing him along.
Someone is walking through a party to get to the front door,
to take a mind clearing walk through the woods,
meeting a deer with spots that were inverted freckles of their own,
that made them realize,
they are beautiful too.
Maybe a lover misheard 'I love it' as 'I love you' and said it back,
unafraid in the moment of what would happen next,
because that joyful mystery,
was what they'd been waiting for.
Perhaps a soul that had been walking the earth just got released,
and that 'it's 5 O'clock somewhere' was reserved for celebrating-

the end of a shift instead of just getting drunk.
All the imperfect rhymes went unnoticed,
and credit was given where it was due.
The spirits were acknowledged and told they
were too important to be invisible,
when they were alive,
but that their joyful mystery lived on.
If I were a positive person,
I'd say all of this to the people I needed to,
instead of telling hard truths,
about relationships, death, sadness and ghosts.
Through ink, and blood, and skin, and water.
Maybe the positivity will come through
someone else,
their ideas and what they pray for,
whether the sorrowful mysteries moved them,
or if they only sing along to rock operas instead
of praying.
If I were a sorrowful person just this once,
I'd say that the joyful mysteries make me feel
like it's 5 O'clock somewhere,
because it's the only rosary I can say at night,
even when I thought I'd done well,
by walking through a party and into the woods,
to see my reflection through animals and lovers,
that were really only one and the same,
when 'I love it' really only meant sex,
and 'I love you' was taken back,

while my hands were as numb as my brain as I
counted my fingers,
as if they were the tenth bead,
and I wasn't beautiful even though I was
invisible.

Praise and Perspective

Good things are understated,
not always pairing those feelings,
like too many cups of coffee,
or entire coconut cream pies.
It's been easy to judge others,
while I try and create myself,
I write and edit full of hope,
finding something from opinions,
the unseen draw of comparison.
I pretend I am a reincarnation,
becoming every big tragic artist.
Who will read what I've made,
perhaps just my loved ones?
My humble audience in analysis;
they imagine they know me,
thinking on about my words,
keeping a lamp on before bed.
I complain they're too helpful,
resentfully expecting guidance,
when I remember I'm a child.
Sometimes clarifying with shampoo,
expecting to clear my head as well,
understanding I need a break,
from the whimpers of my daughter.
I can admit I search for this,

all your praise and perspective,
I accuse you much too often
of aiding those in front of me,
I have lived demanding and using,
never appreciating enough.
I will continue to apologize,
if you stand to educate me.
Though I underpay myself,
and idolize some of your fears,
I promise your importance,
has somehow made me a mother.
It's not all about being helplessly in love,
or handwriting all on my arms and legs,
covering me with temporary tattoos.
I wake up on the couch now,
instead of being carried to bed,
full from coffee and coconuts.
Why couldn't I have thanked anyone,
for turning off the light?
I want you to know I'm fine and alive,
and writing because of you.

www.ingramcontent.com/pod-product-compliance
Lightning Source LLC
Chambersburg PA
CBHW051740130826
49812CB00033B/941
* 9 7 8 9 3 9 5 8 9 0 4 2 7 *